You and Me

A *Love Letter* To *God*

Victoria Brahe-Wiley

BALBOA
PRESS
A DIVISION OF HAY HOUSE

Balboa Press books may be ordered through booksellers or by contacting:

Balboa Press
A Division of Hay House
1663 Liberty Drive
Bloomington, IN 47403
www.balboapress.com
1 (877) 407-4847

Because of the dynamic nature of the Internet, any web addresses or links contained in this book may have changed since publication and may no longer be valid. The views expressed in this work are solely those of the author and do not necessarily reflect the views of the publisher, and the publisher hereby disclaims any responsibility for them.

The author of this book does not dispense medical advice or prescribe the use of any technique as a form of treatment for physical, emotional, or medical problems without the advice of a physician, either directly or indirectly. The intent of the author is only to offer information of a general nature to help you in your quest for emotional and spiritual well-being. In the event you use any of the information in this book for yourself, which is your constitutional right, the author and the publisher assume no responsibility for your actions.

Any people depicted in stock imagery provided by Getty Images are models, and such images are being used for illustrative purposes only.
Certain stock imagery © Getty Images.

Interior Image Credit: Tiffany G. Matthews & Kristin Jo Freed

Scripture quotations marked NIV are taken from the Holy Bible, New International Version®. NIV®. Copyright © 1973, 1978, 1984 by International Bible Society. Used by permission of Zondervan. All rights reserved. [Biblica]

Print information available on the last page.

ISBN: 978-1-9822-3432-4 (sc)
ISBN: 978-1-9822-3433-1 (e)

Balboa Press rev. date: 09/12/2019

This book is dedicated to
Tiffany as consultant, editor, and artist and
Bob as advisor and as Attorney at Law
in gratitude for the tireless wisdom, talents, and support
of these two people
I will never be able to repay.

Acknowledgments

I am grateful for the kindness of Tara Atkins,
who created the path to this book,
and to Jeremy Carey, who made this book divine.
So many other individuals at Balboa Press
helped me publish this first and last book.

Tiffany Matthews' beautiful art
is shown throughout this book.

Everything written in this book is intended
as comfort and devotion, not
proposed to challenge or replace the
reader's inner wisdom.

Contents

Beginning Salutation to You.. xiii

1. Our Beginning 1
2. First Job 7
3. Year of Disasters.. 11
4. Your Version of Interviewing.. 17
5. England, Scotland, and Wales.................................. 21
6. Job at a University.. 25
7. Your Gift of Role Models...................................... 31
8. Mother and Her Trees... 35
9. Popa and Me... 39
10. Miracle at My Desk 41
11. Leaving One Home for Another 45
12. Last Job... 49
13. Your Spiritual Advisors 55
14. Journey from Anger to Forgiveness 59
15. Happy and Unhappy World from You 65
16. 9/11 For Us All 71
17. Death as I Understand It............................... 79
18. Your Teachings of Oneness 83
19. Seeing You Over a Lifetime.......................... 89

Closing Sentences to You... 93

My Beloved Lord,

When I realized I wanted to write a letter of gratitude for Your many teachings of this life, I knew this entire message has to be for You. You are the only one I even begin to relate to within the past two years.

Your love, humor, teachings, and wisdom the past few years have made me joyous, a state of mind I never imagined I would have all those years when I thought I was a separate, solitary self. Now I experience over and over enormous gratitude that this loneliness will never come back.

But to You and with You, I would like to bring some of the stories You created about Our past together. These stories, not in sequence, cover a broad span of years with a lot about Our work life because that is what We did for a very long time to the exclusion of other things.

I am happy You saved these life experiences so I could go back and see Your loving hands outstretched. I trust Your judgment that thinking of being quite different from You and solitary was the right wisdom for all that time.

Love is patient and kind;
Love is not jealous or boastful;
it is not arrogant or rude.
Love does not insist on its own way;
it is not irritable or resentful;
it does not rejoice at wrong,
but rejoices in the right.
Love bears all things, believes all things,
hopes all things, endures all things.
Love never ends ···

1 corinthians 13:4-8

Love is Always the Answer

Our Beginning

1

I do not remember any problem connecting with You as a little girl. You were right on my left side every night where I turned to You facing the wall in the dark. I visualized Your face and shoulders quite clearly, slightly brown skin with that soft expression in Your eyes and Your loving smile just at the corner of Your mouth.

I have never seen Your face with any other expression except the period of this life I imagined You were disappointed in me. But that was years away from my childhood.

The thought of You having moods, some not so nice, turned me away from books like *The Old Testament* of *The Bible* as a child. I could not imagine You being cross with anyone. I listened later in *Bible* classes when I went to school to hear the teachers say that You were really crabby and sometimes even worse.

I knew better because I had seen Your face. Now I know Your face was in my mind's eye. I was nervous when I retired and started an intense study of Your holy books that Your face would change in me. But because You are who You are, I should not have given this fear any thought.

What was loveliest about these years I never for one moment thought You were not right beside me. I could tell by the tilt of Your head, You were always listening. What I remember most is talking Your ears off. In these sharing moments, no one else existed.

You gave me an older sister two and a half years older than me. I headed right for her as soon as I could focus. It was probably neat that she wasn't attached to me. I copied her every move. I am sure it was joyous that I had no idea what she would do.

As recorded in my baby book by my mother, my first sentence was something my sister had said. To this day, I still write with my left hand having copied my sister when we were both little girls. But, in my defense, we lived on a 525 acres farm with very few children visitors to influence me otherwise.

I remember seeing in a large magazine that a very young girl had given birth to a baby. That night, I am sure I began to haunt You on the subject of my having a baby too. I expressly told You I knew this would hurt, but I was willing to go through this in exchange for a sister who would play with me without going off somewhere or ever being mad at me.

You spoiled me early because so much of my childhood was in a natural setting on this farm. The driveway was a mile long, lined with trees toward the entrance on the road. I think it became ordinary to me that there were pear, apple, and cherry trees with the aroma from flowers before these trees gave birth to fruit. There was even asparagus growing wild just within the wooden, rail fence enclosing our large front yard.

Our father grew vegetables every spring, so I grew up with a healthy diet that I couldn't reject fast enough as an adult. All these beautiful proofs of the loveliness of nature became commonplace to me. I can barely remember how beautiful this farm must have been to every person who came to visit.

Popa, who studied and wrote books, had his own office, a small building attached to the main house connected by an open breezeway. My sister and I adored him. Sometimes we would quietly go in his office waiting to hear if there would be a short, welcoming sentence from our father.

Popa printed two volumes of his research books on his press. He was a talented man in many respects. My sister and I believed our father could do anything. We knew he loved fun.

Popa bought and created marionettes. He built a stage for my sister and me to act his stories in front of my parents' friends. I did not realize this was my first experience in public speaking. I was too young to be nervous, and pleasing our father and mother were uppermost in our minds.

As I grew older, I turned more of my attention toward my parents. I began to notice that Popa ended many requests for fixing or helping with toys and gadgets with, "If I am still here." I started to hear this tagged-on sentence about three years before he died, and this worried me. I do not remember if I shared that worry with You.

The morning on the day of his death, his response to my request to fix a toy was the same disqualifier add-on sentence which had caused me to worry. Somehow his response then made me angry, a feeling I was not supposed to have, much less show. I do remember letting the screen door slam behind me, having been trained to cushion this door with my hand to prevent it from making a loud noise.

My father shot himself that night. I was ten years old, my poor sister was thirteen, and our mother had just turned forty years of age a few months before he died. I often thought years later, this horror happened at terrible ages for my sister and mother.

As I watched every person I loved weep to the marrow of their bones, I cried with them. But no amount of touching my grandmother's hands or saying sweet things to my grandfather did any good whatsoever. We were all locked in intense shock and grief.

Momma wrote by hand Popa's funeral service for his body's burial on a section of the farm next to a burial ground already established by previous owners. Her service for Popa ended with, "Goodnight Sweet Prince."

I was so locked mentally into my feelings and everyone else's sadness that I do not remember going to You for comfort or even asking for an explanation of Popa's choice of death.

Because this death was suicide happening in the 1950s, I saw only the closest adult friends of my parents at that funeral. I wondered why everybody else was doing something else they considered more important than helping to comfort my sister, my grandparents, and my mother.

My mother retreated into her holy books, and I am sure she was right with You. All anyone of us needed to be is the awareness of You. There seemed to be no explanation for his choice of death. Even though believing his decision to leave his life was impulsive, this hypothesis did not bring any comfort. But for me, the period of our nightly chats had come to an end several years before.

You did not answer the question of "why" for many years, long after my grandparents had died. Maybe, I should have haunted You for this answer, but I think I was so distracted by the people I loved being overwhelmed with grief that I forgot You.

But that first day back in school on Tuesday after Popa died on Saturday, I remember no teacher or schoolmate said anything to me about my father no longer being here. Their silence was very strange to me because whenever I was out sick, the day I got back to school, lots of people asked how I was feeling.

The one person who even came near me in a consoling manner was the secretary to the principal. She came over to me when I was waiting in line at the cafeteria for lunch and touched my shoulder. I remember being embarrassed that some classmate might notice such an important person paying attention to me. But because I still remember her dark blue dress, her white-collar and the sweet sadness on her face, that touch must have meant the world to me.

I know You touched all of us often. Held us. It is a source of sadness to me that I was not aware of the many times You held my hand. I know You repeatedly did because now I see the love that is You. There must have been so many times You took my palm, but I did not feel this enough to curl my fingers around Yours experiencing safety and relief.

But I do remember Mother told me later she telephoned a doctor friend of theirs right after she saw my father's inert body. This man came immediately. I felt this same doctor rush right to my side as I was walking alone away from Popa's grave And just like You, he held my hand all the way back to our house.

First Job

2

I dropped out of my four-year college because I became overwhelmed with the amount of learning I no longer knew, which I certainly must have learned in those first two years. The only sentence I could remember in German was that I was hungry.

I could not sleep at all. Night after night, I listened to the chimes of the school cathedral clock in the distance hearing every strike of this clock sadder with each hour. I panicked and left. It was almost two decades before You explained the cause of all this.

I did not learn any saleable skill in high school, and the only one I learned in this college was operating a switchboard. I vaguely remember my first interview as being one of bodily strain. I seemed to recall being numb from the neck down, and as I entered the multi-story building of my job request, I now believed I knew nothing about anything any longer.

The man I interviewed with was maybe ten years older than I was. He was very soft, laidback, and he made it easy for me to reply to his questions. I think I love this man to this day. Oddly enough, he hired me.

After dropping out of college, I had moved into an apartment with another girl in her hometown who attended and dropped out of the same college a year before I did.

With this job at a large insurance company, things seemed calm enough for me not to panic. But, abruptly my new roommate moved out in a very few months, having rented an apartment without even telling me.

I became overwhelmed by living alone for the first time. From this point, I imagined myself to be alone. I had no idea what I should do to make myself happy. I remember repeatedly staring out of the back window with a glass of watered-down bourbon at an alley below feeling alone, hopeless, and thoroughly depressed.

Most of the women with whom I worked on this two-position switchboard lived with their families. But You did give me one single woman a few years my senior in age who was an enormous help to me because she had already lived alone for about five years. To my relief, she had acquired lots of experience about how to live alone without feeling lonely.

When I never solved the feelings of loneliness and depression, this older, wiser friend suggested I go to the prestigious secretarial school within blocks of my apartment. She reasoned with much more significant jobs, I might meet people not living exclusively with their families who would become part of my life. My learned friend also pointed out I could later move to other cities of my choice.

Now I am sad to think that then I did not remember You were part of every phase of my life. But feeling alone had its purpose. I would never treasure what We have now had it not been for those years I imagined I was alone.

I studied as I never had before. I still fold letters to go into envelopes as taught at that school. In retirement, I began using shorthand even though it is rusty. But for some unknown reason, I do enjoy using shorthand to write notes to myself.

The teachers of the school elected to give me a passing grade in timed typing tests because, in my other classes, I had earned good grades. But because I always panicked near the end of the document I was typing. I could not even earn a passing grade for these timed typing tests. This fear of typing, making mistakes near the end of the report, stayed with me until I started typing on a computer keyboard decades later.

By living alone, You have taught me that silence can be an excellent teacher. Being focused in my mind in a quiet apartment allowed me to hear within many things I would have missed. I now know all that wisdom which came so gently was from You. You never forced any thought on me, nor did You demand anything. You, unknown to me, were my inner Professor.

I had dated one man when I started living alone in this city. Finally, I realized my boyfriend of three years was never going to marry me because he still lived with his mother, who made the final decision for every aspect of his life. She tolerated me.

Imagining that You left decisions entirely to me, I did not consult You or anyone about my sudden, potentially dangerous decision to move to another city. Maybe family and friends would have told me good reasons not to make this sudden change, but I did not take any chances of being enlightened by asking them.

I had read somewhere that there were readily available jobs with the city I chose to move to because this city currently had an unemployment rate of 4%. I did not know the atmosphere of this city was to its resident noticeably tense and angry due to the assassination of Dr. Martin Luther King, Jr. the year before. A year later, when I started living there, a volatile environment still existed primarily in the African American residential parts of this city. But this tension seemed to me to be citywide.

Not knowing any of this, I did notice riding on buses while looking for a job and an apartment that everyone in expensive suits was avidly studying money magazines. Because I considered myself not shrewd enough to understand these publications, I didn't bother to buy any. Looking back at that coming year, I should have read every magazine in front of me on those buses.

None of the anxious expressions of those reading economic magazines around me entered my consciousness as worry. In one week, I secured a job and an apartment I loved. I was too busy congratulating myself with what I viewed as an enormous success to give You any thought, much less credit. I now saw myself as an independent, career-minded, to-be-successful woman. But this perception did not last for any length of time. In truth, I was still very immature and very frightened.

But You must have steered significant portions of my unusual, exciting work life. When I remember this period of my life, I know You gave me the strength and energy to keep going in the face of so much uncertainty and change.

Year of Disasters

3

My first position of work in this unusual year was as a secretary in an international consulting firm. I talked my way into this job when the woman behind the desk said, "I don't think we have a position for you." She said this because of my schooling in secretarial work, which included shorthand.

I immediately shot back at her, "Oh, yes, you do. I am not overqualified. I would love the position you just described."

The woman, who had interviewed me and to whom I would report, became a life-long friend. She was someone I admired and liked immensely. I tried to follow her example as a woman who did not stop being very feminine no matter how high she rose in rank within this organization.

She promoted me into a position which was called "accountant." Anyone who was a trained and experienced accountant would have laughed at my having this title judging by the work I was performing. I was scared to death because I knew nothing about this subject.

This esteem able lady and I worked closely together in my tiny windowless office preparing numbers of income and expenses for the top manager. He wanted these numbers ahead of the real figures from the New York Office, which came the second week of the month. These two weeks of this delay every month were just too long a period for this impatient manager to wait for monthly numbers. He wanted the profit and loss numbers as soon as the month closed.

Looking back on this, I see that we weren't keeping two sets of books, but it felt like that. Our numbers, it seemed to me, were ridiculous compared to the numbers from the corporate office accountants' profit and loss figures.

But nobody seemed to notice or care about that but silent me saying nothing. Somehow preparing these errors day after day, month after month broke my spirit. I was still immature for my age and very lofty. My ego wanted to prepare accurate reports, even if I was not an accountant.

Having worked for this employer for six whole months, I thought nothing of going right back to the personnel agency which had placed me with this consulting firm. I was happy and grateful the job placement ladies were glad I came back. I know I did not ask You about the resignation. But next, You did assign me to a very unusual position.

It was with an aggressive investment firm, which still exists today. The interview was memorable because it happened in another company's tiny office, which for unknown reasons, had squares of mirrors covering the entire wall facing the interviewer and me.

The same-age-as-me man interviewing me could not take his eyes off himself in that mirror. I got in the habit of clearing my throat to remind him I was there. The position was as his assistant "selling tombstones."

I had not one inkling what that phrase meant, so I approached my first day of work with an immense, specific, tangible amount of fear. For my second job this year, I had no idea of how to do it or any clear concept of what it was. I had taken a role which I had no business accepting. But being unformed emotionally, I quietly tried to assure myself that all would be well. But that assurance never reached the core of my being.

It was clear as soon as I started that there was nothing to do. Mercifully, the telephone never rang. I never had to invent something about tombstones. Three male bosses, including the mirror fiend, with me and one other secretary, held a one-room fort again with no windows.

The other secretary had been with these three men in their previous jobs in a small town with this growing company. She knew them quite well as would-be playboys. I began to believe these men were imagining loopholes in their marriage vows and taking on this big, famous city in noticeable ways.

But in this job, life picked up in an unforeseeable way. Within days my mirror-loving boss, the drop-dead gorgeous one who ruined it all by knowing perfectly well he was just that, sidled slowly up to my desk, stuffed something relatively large and white in my lap under my desk. His only words on this subject _now or ever_ were, "See what you can do with that."

I knew better than to take whatever it was to hold up for the other three people to see, but my curiosity was intense. On one edge, I saw a man's white shirt decorated with lipstick. I casually went to the ladies' room and began to learn a brand-new, relatively-unheard of skill.

I do not recall the number of shirts I received in the next few months without comment from either one of us. This first memorable laundry day I ended up with pink all over the collar. Because I was sure he was married, I knew I had to get this shirt in some ideal shape to be taken home for his wife to bring to the laundry or dry cleaners.

That first garment I tried for hours to render into a spotless, sinless shirt. But with real anxiety, I ended up with a pink embossed collar. This mess of pink smear was the best I could produce.

Immediately after work, I went to the grocery store and almost attacked a spray bottle claiming to remove spots by lifting any stain off the fabric for easy removal. For the next season of life, I was never without this wonderful, very effective spray in the bottom drawer of my desk.

I was so naïve that I thought the subsequent lipstick stains were all from the same person. I wanted to suggest, "Why don't you tell her to take off her lipstick as soon as you meet?!"

Months later, I began to realize the red/pink stains never seemed consistent. I assumed in my naïve, mechanical way that different stains on all these shirts were happening due to impact. I reasoned kisses could be gentle as well as emphatic.

When orange lipstick showed up, I was hit forcefully by an undeniable fact. Different women had implanted these lip-stick stains. That did it. I went right back to my beloved, twice-used personnel agency.

The employees of the agency expressed concern I had come to them two times already in one year. But these women sent me on another interview, and I received yet another job. Gorgeous was very sorry when I told him I was resigning. I did leave the miracle spray in my bottom drawer out of sheer sympathy and kindness to my successor.

Only this time I hit a real low with a thoroughly depressing job. As secretary to a just-promoted man of a national accounting firm, I had absolutely nothing to do. My boss was always back home, half the country away, trying to persuade his wife to move to the city of his new job. Two months later, the fatal telephone call came to me that his wife was not ever going to move, and all discussions with my boss on this subject had come to an end.

I went right back to the employees of my personnel office. Now, these staff members were beginning to worry about *their* reputation. But as You would have it, I got the fourth job in the same year as a secretary working for yet another national accounting firm. To my sorrow, this boss was in the office all the time.

Looking back, I had served in three jobs in one year, and oddly enough all of these companies exist today. I had been sending myself alarm bells ever since the lipstick-ridden shirts, but I was too paralyzed to listen even to myself. It took years to realize that what I was doing was reacting to everything, not planning and executing anything. My whole mindset was to "get another job."

In this new job, there was a firm rule that letters and all other documents had to be typed letter-perfect no matter how many times the poor secretary had to retype them. This office rule had to have been invented by some cruel, idiot man who had never seen, much less touched, a typewriter.

I spent several days of paralysis from the elbows down when I got near the end of a document. This rule created the same fear I experienced in secretarial school with timed-typing tests.

I knew there had to be a way around this sadistic, mentally unhealthy rule. With a small knife from home, I sharpened to a workable point an eraser that fit snuggly on top of the end of my pencil. Gently I removed all offending typing mistakes without a trace. After all, it was a costly bond paper. Anything on it should come off it!

Eventually, I knew perfectly well from where this solution had come. You had created my lipstick removal days for this job. This prior experience was just Your touch for disobeying the orders regarding typing. But I was surprised that I was quite adept at this covert procedure

It would have been impossible to hide what I was doing with the shaved eraser, but later, I did not care. It was a ridiculous rule, and I had no intention of honoring it anymore.

Here I was in another windowless office just large enough for three people and their desks. There were two other secretaries who, like me, had no time to communicate, much less become friends. They often noticed, of course, what I was doing and in a short space of time, they promptly followed.

Having no experience with removing varying shades of every color of lipstick from a white shirt, they sometimes smeared the expensive letterhead paper, and because of obedience to this horrible rule, they had to start typing the letter all over again.

I had no such problem and I made it a point to teach these two now-friendly cohorts carefully. Now, these two women were having great success, not having to retype any document.

I was the Nancy Drew of that firm. My invention quickly spread around the entire secretarial staff, including the secretary of the managing partner. I believed myself to be operating entirely on my own. I was outrageously proud for the whole of the maneuver. I gave You no credit at all.

But with four jobs in the same year, my resume now looked fictional. I finally listed all my skills in bullet form with the names of my employers at the bottom. Putting the same year four times was highly unusual. Putting these repetitive years on a resume advertised my inability to stay at a job.

While my experience and skills were still tangible, they had become unsaleable. In the fourth job, even with the sharp erasers, I had to stay in this job no matter how much I disliked it. And looking back, I believed even then I had created this entire mess all by myself.

But I learned this whole experience had a purpose. It was much later that I realized You were training me in experiences I would need in future jobs in this life. You are, after all, a master Planner.

Your Version of Interviewing

4

*L*ooking back, I certainly understand why You taught me to interview early in my working life. So much of my adult life was nothing but working for some corporation or non-profit.

You taught me I was a person meeting a person. To be paralyzed with fear began to feel abnormal. I looked upon these interviewers with real interest. If they did not want to hire me, perhaps that was for my best interest. So, fear began to melt away.

I noticed these men and women's humanness. Some of them were uncomfortable because they had been drafted into doing this session, leaving their work undone. I began to always ask about that, and being emphatic if they were experiencing that kind of pressure. Asking about this possibility endeared me to these people in an unusual way.

It became so important to me that this interviewer perceived me as an equal. Sometimes with controlling people, creating that as the atmosphere took work on my part. But saying things like, "I know you value organization. So do I," usually helped that person thaw a little and see me as a comrade.

With the cocky, it was different. I had to bring these people's attention back over and over about why we were in this room together. Somehow reminding them their objective was to know me was not always easy. Many of these people wanted to have fun at my expense.

But I did meet very human people. And with them, I was a lot more interested in the job they were trying to fill. If this person across from me was quite mortal and had stayed that way within their employment, the chances were if I became an employee, I would remain a person too.

But the worst were the interviewers who were out to prove something. During one interview a lawyer rewrote my resume. I knew long before he finished that it would be misery to work for him, and I could hardly wait for him to finish so I could get up and leave without a word.

Even with Your wonderful training, so much of interviewing was trial and error. I never made the mistake of talking down to the person interviewing me. But I did experience massive put-downs from some interviewers. When that happened, again, all I wanted to do was leave.

I think it was Your teaching of kindness that leveled the playing field more than anything. You are a pro at kindness, and You showed me often that this was exactly the emotion You wanted for my current situation.

I think interviewing has such an ominous reputation because the outcome is so uncertain. For the part of me that seeks to control the unknown or the current happening, I saw over and over how truly helpless I was in this respect. But years later, I knew I was far from helpless with You overseeing.

But, with Your help, I had obtained four jobs in the same year in the city where I had just moved. Those experiences helped to let me realize we are people among people. I began to turn the situation around in my mind, which helped me focus enormously.

Was this person dressed appropriately for this interview? Did they smoke (in those days,) drink or eat in front of me without offering the same to me? I watched one man consume his entire lunch thinking nothing of it. He struck me as a very sad, isolated person.

Did this person complain about their staff or the company they represented? I was always so surprised that anyone would make that mistake. Did they like their job? Was I comfortable with this interviewer?

And last, but hardly least, if I were doing the hiring, would I want to have this person as my employee?

You taught me the importance of respect. If I did not have it for this interviewer, then I did not belong in that company. Knowing that I respected this interviewer and would hire them made enormous differences within my mind.

But what I have talked about so far was equally true for non-profit organizations. Painfully I learned that some very nice people could turn out to be unethical. Being employed by some of those organizations, I was appalled that my bosses had no shame in their actions and expected me to go right along with them. Being employed by a non-profit organization did not quarantee this company had integrity.

But You taught me the real skill of interviewing is making an analysis of the person I met and any observations I could take in of the company in the very beginning. The mood of the receptionist was important. Getting snarled at by this person said a lot about her relationship to this company and probably how this organization treated her. The condition of the furniture said something about how that company treated those within its employment.

You showed me over and over, it was the little things that bore evidence of who these employers were before I ever met the interviewer. And I learned to value what You were clearly showing me.

That doesn't mean I made all the right choices. But I now know You well enough to know You wasted no part of those years of employment. You are a good teacher, and I thank You over and over for your patience.

We are Truly One

England, Scotland, and Wales

5

One time when You and I were not working on a job, my niece asked me to go with her and her class for a guided tour abroad. I was thrilled she asked me. As it turned out, I learned an enormous amount about her, about You and me.

This trip was 4 years before I knew about the mental disorder that had affected me since college. The things I remember about this trip make me sad when I think of my behavior. I realize I kidnapped my niece.

I remember talking to her on the plane going over. Everything seemed fine then. But when we landed in London, we were put on a bus. That bus sat there for more than an hour.

I remember becoming numb. I remember being enormously frightened because I had not had this symptom before. The longer we were waiting on that bus, the worse my condition became.

At the hotel, I remember my niece and I were by ourselves at the desk of the man assigning rooms. At least I hope we were by ourselves. When the clerk said my niece would be in another room from me, I lost all control. I remember screaming at him, and eventually him yelling at me. But he did change our room assignments so I would be with my niece.

When we got to our room, I remember saying I needed to lie down. Immediately I knew this wasn't going to relieve any of my symptoms which by now were varied and worse.

Mercifully enough, I do not remember much of this trip. But I do remember always sitting with my niece wherever we were. And I remember her not talking to her classmates. I had her hostage, and I am sure it showed. After my screaming at the desk clerk, I am sure my niece was hoping and trying to make sure that didn't happen again.

Most of that trip is an entire blank. I had no idea what was wrong with me, and I was intent upon hiding it from everyone, including my niece. I tried so hard to be normal. I remember one breakfast in England. My niece was looking at her classmates. Maybe it was my imagination, but I seem to remember a wistful expression on her face.

I do remember saying I was going to stay on the bus in Wales. We were nearing the end of our trip, and now I had so many symptoms of mental and physical disorder, I no longer could identify them all.

I have always wished I could take that trip over with my beloved niece. But You don't make things that way.

I remember going to my mailbox and seeing a picture from my niece. It was of a little sheep grazing in a field. We had seen so many sheep together in fields. But her color picture contained only one. I remember hoping that little sheep was her.

To me, this picture represented enormous forgiveness and understanding. My niece continued for the next twenty-five years to send me pictures made by her. My mailbox became my heaven. She never stopped.

Now I see that little sheep quite differently. This lovely image is my niece, me and You. There is an undying unity of the three of us and with the whole world. You have left no one out. That picture will always touch my heart.

I saw on that trip and after years of enormous courage and open-heartedness of my niece. Then and now, she is a role model of compassion and love. Thank You, Beloved, for Your gift of her. Thank you with all my heart.

Job at a University

6

You even gave me a husband with whom I moved to a university town when I was still in my twenties. As a complete surprise to me, I was offered a position in the university's Bursar's Office. Now I had enough accounting experience to qualify. And I was the wife of an assistant coach whose position must have also been in my favor. I had never worked for a school of any size before, and I was looking forward to this job.

There were lots of unhappy events ahead of me. Now I am just grateful to You that I was never alone with these problems. At the time, I felt chiefly confident, but alone.

Initially, I met with the controller who advised me I would be reopening an abandoned tuition program. I was sure that I would enjoy the job and learn all kinds of new skills from it in this non-corporate environment.

On my first day of this assignment, I met my immediate boss who by his looks was even younger than I was. In my previous jobs, my supervisors were older. Now I wondered if this younger man knew as clearly as the controller had what I would be facing while performing this job.

My first day, sitting at my new desk surrounded by many overflowing cardboard boxes, my new immediate boss explained that all this material was a tuition postponement project. I had been hired to restore this program to an active state. These files had been in some school attic pending a supervisor's arrival. I must have looked significantly uneasy because my boss made a great effort to impress upon me that everything would be fine. He said I just needed to "sort it."

Several months later, I realized my boss was completely naïve about what I needed to do to bring this program back to life. "Sort" hardly describes what waited for me in those brimming boxes. On my first day, the very first piece of paper I picked up had no relationship to the piece of paper right below it. I had never in my so-far years of working seen anything remotely resembling this mess.

For a few days, I just aimlessly picked up papers in these full boxes in a total fog, not knowing how to begin. Finally, I came up with categories to separate in piles: general information, contracts signed, and information regarding the students on the list for this program. I tried to remember, which I am sure You taught me, that not knowing how to do something may not necessarily be permanent.

I had expected to find multiple contracts with parents' signatures, but there were none. The students themselves signed for this commitment, and 100% of these no-longer students at the university obviously had never graduated. This temporary free-ride was supposed to be paid back to the university after graduation. But this program had not received any payments. All the students in my files had dropped out of this prestigious, academic haven.

One weekend I took home all the files I could carry regarding the students who had signed for this program and received money toward tuition. On Saturday, I stalled and fretted about calling them. My husband pointed out that I wasn't selling anything. I was merely reminding them of an unpaid debt. He affirmed that calling them at 9 am Saturday was not unreasonable, even when they had never heard from the university before.

Having been encouraged by my spouse, I placed my first call to an Ashram in a large city where a young tuition defaulter man now resided. How I knew this unlikely residence must have come from my large boxes of papers. Looking back, every person in this study had to leave an address and telephone number when they withdrew from the university. These pieces of paper were worth everything to me because there was no subsequent information anywhere on anyone.

I had carefully tracked down every available telephone number for my signees. I was entirely ready on that Saturday morning with my rehearsed speech about legal commitment, responsibility, and future payments.

This university was exclusively men. Every phone number was incorrect in my files, but I tracked down phone numbers with tiny bits of information based on last known addresses, using detective skills I didn't know I possessed.

When I reached the Ashram, I quickly asked to speak with the person whose name I had carefully rehearsed. The lady answering the phone told me his name was Mishramananda, which threw me because her pronunciation seemed to go on a long period of time. Mishramananda did come to the phone, and after my canned synopsis, he informed me he was committed to following Krishna and all debts from his previous life were utterly canceled. In other words, as he continued to speak, his positive assessment was that I didn't have a legal leg on which to stand.

He wished me a blissful life and hung up. I think I held the phone to my ear for another ten seconds while I tried to absorb that pronouncement. I knew nothing about Krishna, but I did wonder what he would think of a deliberate unpaid debt.

My next call was not to a religious organization but to an individual, who obviously had been asleep when his telephone rang. This sleepy former-student clearly could not take in who I was or what organization I represented.

When his mind did come to the surface enough to realize the nature of my call, he confidently informed me that he wasn't working, had never worked, and probably would never work, so the owner of the debt was "simply out of luck forever." I wondered where the financial support came for his current residence. I had made two telephone calls and obtained two zeros for any hope of monetary reimbursement.

The rest of the morning had the same results. By noon I was utterly disheartened. There was absolutely no hope for any success in my new job. At my lowest moment, I heard my husband say, "You did your best. That's enough." Why was I having such a hard time internalizing those reassuring sentences?

Monday at my desk was not cheery either. I carefully documented each telephone call, the working, hard-found telephone number, and the conversation as word-to-word as I could remember it. I was far from the "blissful life" the Ashram member wished for me.

You were right with me, but again, not knowing this, I felt very alone.

No one was asking about the program, much less my progress. I do not remember how long it took me to realize that my next and only step was to write a synopsis of everything I had unearthed in the past few months.

It was, in my opinion, pointless to try to find the remaining ex-students. This labor-intensive guide would merely contain all the detective routes for finding lost students which I had learned and a summary of all the fruitless telephone calls I had made. I was not satisfied with this as the logical end to the performance of my position at a prestigious university.

I now knew I was leaving fairly soon because my husband and I agreed to separate. I considered it too early to give my resignation. In this pending-results frame of mind, I proceeded to prepare an evaluation of this program, which left nothing to the reader's ingenuity.

I knew my supervisor and the controller read this document. But I honestly think it was read and understood by even higher-up personnel because later I was told the university closed the postponement of tuition program never to open again. The trustees, I gather, just voted to absorb their losses.

But I had learned that indeed one's best is indeed enough. It has always been enough for You. I tried to remember this truth for the remainder of my working life. I am not my job, the job does not define me, and the job's future has nothing to do with mine. Learning this lesson, this piece of gold, brought me to the blissful state that Mishramananda had wished for me. However, I am sure Mishramananda doesn't know bliss only comes from You.

Your Gift of Role Models

7

 our consciousness has manifested itself in all the generations before me. Early every morning, I pay homage to my ancestors, starting with my grandparents, whom I adored. I learned so much from both my grandmothers and my grandfather. It is Your gift that they lived overlapping my life.

I realize that these people whose pictures are on my wall were five generations of hard-working women and men. I thank these people with an offering of water. I express gratitude for enduring everything they suffered. I thank them for what they gave the world and what they left behind. I believe these people give today through all of the descendants who came after them.

Over so many years of being employed, I had different people to whom I reported. I remember both those I admired, and those I did not. But there are four people, two women and two men who will always be loved by me.

The first woman was the one I mentioned working for in my first job in my disastrous year. She was a role model for my young life. Her graceful femininity always made me grateful I was a woman. For many future years, I saw women lose the best parts of their gender as they struggled up what was then a male ladder. But I also saw many successful women seem more like men when they adopted extreme aggression.

What moved me the most about my first female boss was her kindness. I was a person to her, not just someone she supervised. I met her family as she and I grew closer. She was part of my life, and she made me feel part of hers.

But, over the years, her kindness never stopped. I listed her name as a reference for me for many years. I am sure she was able to describe any virtues I might have had with great conviction.

My second female boss was crucial to me and my wellbeing at many times and in so many ways. I did not realize I was struggling against a crippling illness. The result of this fear was I found it enormously difficult actually to go to work. I was frequently afraid to go with no clear idea of why I was so fearful.

I was working in a private environmental preservation agency as their bookkeeper. In spite of inner terror about being at work, I never missed preparing the payroll on time and distributing paychecks accordingly. I did not pay myself for time not worked. But I was becoming a shadow employee. My poor boss never knew when I was going to be at my desk.

This caring lady refused to let me close the door to my small office when I was alone. She knew I lived alone, and I think she just wanted my work life to be entirely different. But I was convinced everyone I worked with at that firm thought I was crazy. I thought so too.

But no one treated me as though I were mentally unsound. Kindness came from everyone, which oddly enough made my depression worse. So often, I was unable to return these feelings. But I just wasn't in my own body. These people were talking to a shell of a body with no person inside.

My loving boss decided what I needed was to stay with her for a few days. She came to my apartment with me as I packed a few things to stay overnight at her house for that short period.

I guess her theory was if I ate good meals at regular times, slept a full night, and had someone to talk to my mind would improve its sad moods.

I remember sitting with her at night in her spacious den, talking about myself in answer to her questions. But because she was the boss of my only paying job, there was an enormous number of subjects I could not possibly share with her.

What I was feeling in my depression was wanting not to be. I didn't want to commit suicide; my phrase to myself was, "Don't stop the world, just let me off." Sharing with her completely was not possible because my prevailing thought was the idea of wanting to be dead without taking any action.

Somehow, I managed to move to another city near where my sister and her family lived, her husband having been promoted and transferred to that area. Tagging after my sister and moving everything I owned to be with her made me hopeful. But, in less than a year, my brother-in-law was promoted again, this time back to a small town he and my sister had lived when their two daughters were first born.

Even though I never actually lived with my sister after she went to college, I often called over many years to tell her my sad feelings, as though saying these statements would make them less painful.

But, when my sister and her family left the large city I had moved to be with her, I was left alone in a way I had never been before. I had lived in my apartment for less than a year and was experiencing the terror of going to work all over again.

But this time I could see Your hand stretching out over my life. My supervisor for this office manager job of mine was located in another large city half of this country away. So even though I am sure my rotten attendance to my post was reported to him by thoroughly annoyed co-workers, this man never seemed to be even slightly irritated with me.

I am sure I lamented to him that my sister and her family had moved away. This wonderful man spread the canopy of caring about me soon after I found myself alone in this strange city. After my sister moved away, he said on the telephone, "How would you like to move up in the world?"

My rescuer authorized payment to move me to the city in which he worked. He assigned me to work for his assistant who would be preparing the annual budget for this entire large company due in a matter of weeks.

My boss's assistant and I started traveling around the country, visiting offices to determine their financial needs for the coming year. This man was as kind and responsive to me as his boss. I had gone from feeling dreadful to be happy with my new apartment, new job, new supervisor, and my familiar, caring boss.

These two men told me I was smart, and because I admired them so much, I began to think this might be true. They also made it clear I was attractive, another concept I had not entertained for most of my life.

Both of them became my friends. They were role models of excellence: bright, caring for others as well as me, ambitious, and hard-working. I thoroughly enjoyed struggling to be just like them.

Looking back, I have an enormous love for You for giving me these four people to try to pattern myself into being similar to them. They were excellent role models, and their presence in my life certainly helped over and over in my depression to see my world differently and with a more positive approach.

Now You are my boss. I can feel Your supervision when I am writing something that is a memoir like now writing this book. I am aware of Your presence when I work at this desk, sometimes for many hours. I love being Your bookkeeper studiously supervising Your money, Your secretary writing letters and creating original, colorful cards inspired by You. But most of all, I love being Your devotee reading, absorbing and being comforted by all Your holy books and writings. We are together right here.

Writing this book with You, I see so many wonderful times You stepped right in to change, fix, enhance, or adorn the circumstances of this life. Your gifts of the mother, father, sister, role models, and ancestors take my breath away. Your gifts all this life have been lavish.

Mother and Her Trees

8

I was always grateful to You for the mother You gave me. When I was talking Your ears off in bed in the dark as a tiny girl, I wanted You to know how much I loved my mother and how grateful I was to You having her.

I wrote this paper years ago, and I give this to You now.

When my father died, Momma was still young. As she searched in her mind for how to support my sister, me, and herself, she certainly faced her shortcoming. She had two steel pins in her hips from operations in the early 1940s even though such surgeries were almost unheard of at that time.

We all regarded Mother as something of a miracle because she walked without crutches early after the operations in defiance of being told she would never walk again. She accomplished this feat by riding her stationary bike to the sun, moon, and back. At the time of this story, she walked only with a cane.

In her search for supportive money, Momma finally decided to make our farm a tree farm. She knew no one who had done such a thing, but this did not stop my mother. The Forestry Service gave Momma 500 little pine seedlings.

Mother and I took the 500 little pine seedlings and went to a large open field. This day was beautifully sunny, and the fall air invigorated both of us.

I find it hard to believe that we planted 500 little trees that day, but I do remember there was some urgency getting the seedlings into the ground before they died.

My job was to bury a post hole digger as deep as I could in the ground, close the blades and pull up the dirt between the blades. I then put the soil to one side of the open hole.

Mother, however, could not bend over like me, so calmly she crawled and slid along the ground to the gaping hole I had just created. Then she put a little sapling within the hole I just dug and covered it carefully with the dirt I had left to one side. The care and love she showed for each little seedling were very calming to me and renewed my energy to dig another hole with each tree tucked in the ground.

We probably did plant all 500 trees, But I noticed and admired the manner Momma blessed, cared about, and planted these little lifesavers to her finances so repeatedly.

At the end of the day with daylight still shining, I looked closely at my mother. The front of her trousers was utterly gone; only the seam at the very bottom held the pants in juxtaposition to her ankles.

We both laughed and enjoyed our triumph of all these little ones safely in the ground. But for the rest of this life, I hope I never forget her massive stamina shown that day. But her determination sparkling with love, concern, and hope meant my mother was to me a living example of what a physically challenged woman could do. I wanted even then to have that kind of love and commitment to whatever You asked of me this life.

Momma was the first lady tree farmer in the state in which we lived. Looking back, I realize she was the first in all kinds of things.

What a lovely role model of a strong woman You gave me. Thank You, my Beloved, for showing me an example of how to be an accomplished female in what was then a man's world.

Popa and Me

9

It was 33 years before You answered the question of the "why" of my father's choice to leave his life.

I experienced horror meditating on my prayer rug early one Monday morning. A force of energy which felt exactly like a snake shot quickly up my spine and fell back down just as fast. I knew right at that moment I was not the same person. I do not have the words to describe how awful this experience was.

All I could think was, why didn't my meditation teacher warn me?

Over 19 years, I had suffered various confusing symptoms. As I said, after two years in college, I could no longer remember the simplest things I had learned and then became unable to sleep. My body became my enemy. Not knowing how I would feel emotionally, who or when I would hurt or offend, became my definition of insanity. For years I had a little vote on what I would say or do next. Anything could happen very fast. It was terrifying.

At the hospital, the doctors diagnosed that I had bipolar disorder.

Your answer to the "why" of my father's sudden death became apparent as my sister, mother, and I began to remember the last few years of Popa's life. His behavior in those years looked just like mine had been since college.

I had been living in a body like a building always collapsing from within, yet never shutting down completely. I am not critical of anyone who makes this permanent choice. Like many others, I wished I could have saved Robin Williams, the actor, from himself the night he chose to die. I wished that I could have saved my father.

There were reports of Mr. Williams experiencing deep depression like my father and me, which sometimes with me meant I couldn't get out of bed. I became terrified of my jobs and, as I said, often could not go in.

For several years I struggled to feel or at least seem rational and reasonable. I had abandoned You completely. I never even thought about You. It was not that I was angry with You. For me then You didn't exist.

But even then, I did not want to take this life You gave me and vehemently shoved it back in Your face, declaring loudly, "This wasn't enough!" You have taught me a lot about living and dying in the past two years. I am with You in a closeness I never dared to hope.

And I know the night my father died, You scooped him right up in Your arms before the bullet ever left that gun. You are that kind of love.

Miracle at My Desk

10

I did continue using my skills as a secretary. I vividly remember these times were happy ones. But after 3 years of feeling fulfilled, I discovered the working world now regarded secretaries as inconsequential and definitely below most occupations. So, I headed for new talents.

I discovered and learned my to-be-adored trade of bookkeeping from a long-distance course I found listed inside a matchbook cover. I told no one because this course was probably not first-class training. But I knew nothing about bookkeeping. So, I reasoned any school offering training in this trade should be qualified to teach me.

I did not finish the entire course, but I did complete probably two-thirds of it. I remember doing homework and sending it and tests to this course's home office for over a year. I learned enough to know I loved it, but You provided subsequent jobs that taught me this well-loved trade.

Today, I love working for You. I remember how much I loved bookkeeping. Throughout this lifetime, I learned to hate accounting with its mass of numbers and exact procedures which I found annoying, unnerving, difficult, and rigid in the extreme.

But in my new days of bookkeeping jobs, I still believed my life, my money, my happiness, and my success depended entirely on my decisions. And I knew enough from my experiences that I should be afraid of my choices which had turned out so badly in the past. I seemed to be against myself.

I was trying to recover from newly diagnosed bipolar disorder. For two years, I was unemployed. It seems strange now realizing how active You were in my life and how now You showed this beyond doubt. After being without a job for so long, I broke all my prejudices about accounting and was grateful to accept a position after so much lonely time at home.

I, like all the other accountants, was seated in a tiny, fabric cubicle. The one I occupied had a large round ink spot on the fabric directly facing me. I could not imagine how my predecessor managed to spray so much liquid ink in the era of ballpoint pens on that cubicle wall. I also had no idea how his massive spill could have formed a perfect circle.

Not much later, I spilled a small cup of water over my desk. I was shocked when I saw the results on this ink spot. The round ink blot had become the very distinct profile of an angel with her wings just above her.

My eyes filled with tears. After all these lonely years, I realized You were always there, adding wisdom, still helping in so many ways.

The memory I have of Your angel will always remind me of that moment of realizing I am always Home with You.

Just Beyond New Home

Leaving One Home for Another

11

After living almost three decades in the same place, even the same apartment, I was unprepared to being unable to find a job when the church I was working for no longer could afford my services.

Because of my age, no one wanted to hire me envisioning my draining their medical insurance for all my impending needed care. I could not even get a job below my experience, and I was forced to move back to the state in which I grew up.

My medical condition was stable for some time in my previous city. But when I arrived in this new small, rural city where my sister and some of her family lived, I was not even aware of the stabilizing treatment of my chronic disorder. I cannot remember how a doctor I stayed with for 6 years managed to reverse my stabilization.

In this period, I was in what had to be the dark night of the soul. And I had not the slightest idea what was going on or how to amend it. I learned that my doctor was addicted to tobacco, which previously I had never given much thought. But over those years in his care, I experienced a doctor who focused on the larger picture and ignored details.

Looking back, I see Your hand carving out a deeper, wider space within me that You would fill. But then, I just felt lost and terribly depressed. I learned that the 24/7 nurses of my health insurance company were wonderful sources of care, helpful observations and suggestions. Three times I turned to them in a deep depression in the middle of the night, and one of the things these nurses kept saying was, "You have got to get another doctor."

But I felt unable to do this in this small town. And I did like my doctor because I did not blame him for my depression.

That's when I began to realize that people who smoke live in a different mind-set. But, as always, You turned this negative into a positive, and I was given the best doctor at that medical facility. Within weeks he restored me to a stable condition where I have remained ever since.

Living in the same city with my sister, her husband and one of her daughters with her family, I experienced loneliness I had not felt for many years. All of them were sweet and kind, but seldom available.

I am sure my sister was not at all surprised when physiologically I went back, probably within days, to the complete emotional dependence I had always put on her as a child and early adulthood. What I wanted was frequent visits which were one-to-one with my sister and maybe separately her daughter.

My sister knew about a job with a church where a friend of hers worked. My sister had known this woman while playing bridge since both their children were in diapers. I was very grateful to her for lining me up with a job since work was predominately all I had done for many years.

When my sister and this potential boss hugged enthusiastically, I realized having my sister so much in this woman's favor was a definite potential plus for me. In all my working life I had never had such a perk.

My sister's bridge comrade asked if my sister would like to stay while she and I met to discuss this job. To my surprise, my sister sat down on the couch in the parlor where the discussion was to take place. This incident was one of the first things You showed me that everything now was going to be very different from my previous decades of employment.

Having my sister in an interview was unheard of by all my friends left behind in the city of my choice. I wondered if they would believe me if I told them some prospective employer invited a relative of the applicant for this private session. I could not adjust that quickly, but I began to realize that the sooner I accepted that life circumstances now were to be very different, the happier I would be.

This interview was within weeks after I arrived in this tiny city. I quickly saw my sister's friend was going to hire me because my primary character reference and her friend was sitting right there. She seemed kind enough, but I reserved judgment until later. I was in no position to consider turning this job down.

This lady told me in detail what her needs were for an assistant and many of the challenges of this part-time job. I was impressed with her skill of interviewing. She hired me immediately, which was very relieving to me at the time. Thanks to my new boss, my sister, and You I would not be worrying about how to look for a job.

A part-time job was very different from the grueling hours I had worked over much of my stint previously as a paid employee. When three o'clock came, I left. I was delighted with this new, previously unknown, slant on a job.

With the onslaught of deep depression, I was enormously grateful to have a boss and not be in charge of everything. We worked together well, and she even had a good sense of humor about my mistakes. She and I worked in this pleasant relationship for 3 years.

Hiding how I felt was becoming a skill. Depressed just didn't fit with this prestigious church. But, when my boss decided to retire, she did the unthinkable and promoted me to her position.

Now the nightmare of my mental condition started in earnest. My boss had been in her position for many years, and along the way, she learned to take care of anything and everything. I kept running into things I had never done with her, and the incompetence I felt for myself was growing.

Within a year, I knew I had to resign. Looking for another job in a city I was still unfamiliar with frightened me. But, once again, You brought me to a job picked by You where I learned all kinds of things about letting go which was next on Your agenda. Surrender to You was still in the future, but You planted me where I could gently learn more about this needed skill which would bring me to the wonderful truth of You and me.

Last Job

12

I encountered Your influence even more in the job I accepted before this lovely retirement period that is strictly for Us. I do remember thinking I would die at some desk. I just never thought past working.

I know now I have had the same loving boss all these years, and remembering these jobs fills me with happiness as I look back seeing Your constant participation.

After I left the church where I worked in this rural town, I found it difficult to obtain another job in my field. I interviewed with another church, but it was so far from my apartment that I would be paying more money in taxi fares than I would earn working there. I had not needed a car living in a large city previously, and I did not want to resume driving after nearly 30 years.

I was feeling a little desperate after five months at home when I logged on with a government site which listed a CPA firm looking for a bookkeeper. I wrote my usual three-paragraph letter and was surprised to receive a telephone call asking me to come in for an interview.

When I met the owner of the firm, she was a hands-on employer. After talking about the position with questions from me, she announced, "This is how I work. I am offering you the position," and quoted an hourly salary.

I knew that this unusual practice had something wrong. Because I didn't want to spend any more time at home, I accepted the job.

It was a part-time position, just like my previous employment at the church. We agreed on the days and hours I would work. Something was lulling in the back of my mind but not enough to turn the job down.

When I got home that day, I had two negative observations. If she hired me without checking with references to establish my credibility, maybe this instant hire was because she didn't want me to be checking on her business reputation.

The second observation was that the lobby of this CPA firm was completely filled with all Christian items. I had already learned that in this part of the country that meant my new boss was of the faith that did not enjoy the reputation for tolerance of other religions. I had never seen even a church lobby with so many holy items. There was an open *Bible* on the coffee table that had caught my eye the moment I first entered this office which I am sure was intended.

You have taught me well about opposites. Charming, disarming people can be outright crooks. I was wary of people who wore their religion as part of their attire. I had already discovered that an avid Christian might not know or practice the profound principles of their faith.

I was deeply concerned about both of these negative observations. But I felt at the time I had no choice about working for this woman.

My first day she took me in tow. She apologized that I would be in the kitchen because she had more people than offices. I am sure my face reflected the question I was thinking. When we went to the kitchen, the table where I would be sitting was covered with crumbs of food as was the floor.

Pointing to the laptop computer, my boss said, "This will be yours." I immediately said, "Then I will be getting a mouse and a keyboard." I knew all too well how awkward I was handling a laptop with just a small manual space for entry of all data. She looked a little startled and then left the room. I went into the only closet in the kitchen.

Finding a broom, I began sweeping the room. When this new boss came back, she looked a little surprised to see me in my dress suit, which I never wore to this job again, cleaning the kitchen. I did not comment, and neither did she.

My boss left again with neither one of us having said a word. The lady I would report to reentered with a mouse and a keyboard for "my" laptop. She deftly plugged both these attachments into the computer and gave me some files, explaining what she wanted me to do.

I observed initially that this job was a lemon unfit for any human's consumption. I saw my boss now as uncaring about the people who worked for her. I met another woman across the hall from the kitchen and was very happy to have a pleasant, kind human being close at hand.

My relatively new boss assigned me things of drudgery which she didn't like doing. I was happy with this arrangement because these projects meant I would be working independently of her.

But my co-worker across the hall had not shown up for work my second week. The receptionist told me my new friend had been fired. I worried things were already getting out of hand.

The CPA was always very tedious about bringing new employees into the kitchen to meet me. But over the following weeks, I learned that it was pointless to remember the names of the persons to whom my boss introduced me because as an employee, they never lasted very long.

The receptionist and I seemed to be the only ones who were always still left when the latest round of bookkeepers was fired. Later I discovered this receptionist kept a bottle of wine under her desk and consumed its contents as she deemed necessary throughout the day. I was not ready for that - yet.

But I was content. I had work I enjoyed, and that seemed to be all that was important. The parade of employees hired and soon released continued. The state of our actual books was no longer accurate because there were so many different people entering financial information at very different levels of expertise.

But this boss seemed not to be phased by any of this traffic. By now, I was doing projects that I dearly loved, untouched by other short-term staff, and putting up with the said boss was an almost unnoticed part of this job.

Something worrisome dawned on me after about 14 months at that CPA firm. I had worked happily at my kitchen desk on projects which had meaning to me and presumably to clients.

But soon I observed that this office was getting many tax returns refused and sent back by the IRS. My boss, the sole preparer of all tax returns, bragged that she prepared 24 tax returns every night during tax season. That statement alarmed me.

I decided to check via the internet my boss's status as a Certified Public Accountant in the Commonwealth in which she and I lived. The message finally came that there was no listing as a CPA with the name I supplied. I had been working for a phony religious crook.

Shortly after, I said goodbye to the three people there, which included my dishonest boss and quietly left. But I knew deep inside that this position had been a triumph from start to finish solely due to the attitude You taught me toward work. I performed the job to the best of my ability for its own sake.

I did not know then that this was my last paid position. My admired and adored mother died soon after I left this last job. My sister, as executrix, helped me establish funds capable of supporting me while I lived in the retirement my mother wanted.

I did not name all those years of employment as a career. Now I know that any success was entirely due to Your teaching of inner wisdom. And with that knowledge, I was fit for the unexpected retirement You planned for both of Us which included an awareness of You I had never realized before and for which years ago never dared even to hope. These last two years mean the whole wide earth to me.

Your Spiritual Advisors

13

I read Buddhism in retirement. I was fascinated by a "beginner's mind." I experienced all my wretched judgments, facts I had previously imagined expounding to others. Now I see my intent to teach others as ridiculous because all of them have within them my wonderful Professor. I knew the feeling of contentment had to follow just abandoning these ideas and envisioned practices.

The Buddhist concept of every person going through thousands of lives depressed me. You lovingly introduced me to a mentor who had studied and lectured on the Buddhist faith. This man helped me study his religion in depth. But for months reading and hearing no reference to the existence of "God" just made me homesick for You.

Because I knew You were right by my side when I was a little girl, I began to wonder where and why I was not experiencing You now. Studying religions believing in reincarnation, I imagined my first religion in my first life I would emphatically believe my faith was the only one that could be true. Here I would develop a strong ego. And then I imagined I would spend the rest of my lives trying to get rid of this rascal.

For this life, You gave me a spiritual teacher when I moved away from the home I loved so much. In this city, I subsequently experienced deep loneliness which You comforted with a loving person. You even picked her title. I was sitting next to the minister of a small church when suddenly I turned to her and said, "Will you be my spiritual advisor?

The lady on the other side of this minister snapped, "She doesn't even come to church!" My brand-new spiritual advisor turned to me and said, "I'd love to."

I knew even then that she had Your title. I had never heard of a spiritual advisor before it came out of my mouth. I treated her with enormous respect and love. I would invite her to lunch and insist upon paying because I wanted to give her every gift I could possibly afford.

My beloved advisor coached me through the two subsequent employments in this perpetually new-to-me city. Through patience and love, she healed old wounds within me. She envisioned You as rather impersonal, but she had no difficulty with my vision of You as vivid and personal within the depths of me.

I treated her like the gift she was. Looking back, I know You saw my loneliness and gave me this wonderful, dedicated woman to help deal with this emotional pain. I typed significant parts of her self-published book based on articles she had written over the years that appeared in the local newspaper. I enjoyed sitting with her at her book signing party in a local bookstore.

She never called me, but I did not take offense. She did call me once the day before having a stroke which took her life four days later. In that telephone call, we laughed a lot. At her request, I had ordered a print-out of a free natal chart of astrology with her birth date. With humor in her voice, she asked, "Do you think I am vain?" Knowing she always cared about her appearance, both of us dissolved into laughter. She said the trouble with the chart I just sent her was everything on it applied directly to her.

The day she experienced this massive bodily change, my beloved advisor had been a widow for almost a year. Her husband was the kind of man who did everything from preparing the taxes to having their car inspected. My advisor's husband was the one in charge of daily responsibilities, which left this lovely woman free to pursue her faith and later her ministry.

I could see my spiritual advisor now felt like half a person after her husband's death. At our last luncheon together the week before her stroke, I noticed my friend and spiritual coach looking around the room of this restaurant. She had never behaved this way. We always sat in restaurants with our heads close together. So much of the things we discussed were for us alone. Also, she insisted on paying for her meal. I had adopted for the past year surrender to whatever this beloved lady wanted because I could see how unhappy she had been throughout these 12 months.

On my birthday, I learned that she had a massive stroke. I did not ask You to change Your plans for her or me. This pleading was something I had never done as an adult. I saw this stroke Your invitation for her to come home to You. I envied her enormously. I wondered if now she experienced You as entirely personal. Over and over I thanked You for this gift of a devoted listener when You knew I was so lonely. Your choices in this life have always been perfect.

Journey From Anger to Forgiveness

14

*I*n retirement, I had the opportunity to go back to spiritual books I had loved so many years ago. Reading passages referring to subduing and eliminating anger, I started to study emotions and skills to deal with the negative emotions that had plagued me all this life.

My sister and I were not allowed to show anger, and I remember not feeling safe for fear of punishment when this emotion would take over my body. My parents were adamant that we could not wear this emotion on the outside of our bodies. Looking back, maybe this edict was created because my parents found their anger startling.

I think some children hear their parents expressing anger with each other as causes of worry. Later I remembered my parents fought over their sense of right and wrong. If they did not agree on what this constituted, they were angry. But now I do not believe anyone can change another with anger being present.

I have struggled with the feelings of anger all my life. Just like my mother, I seldom show my disagreeable emotion directly to the person. And I know my anger has absolutely nothing to do with my parents' anger. This negative trait is within *me*. This anger is mine and mine alone.

Sometimes I feel hijacked by my mind continually ranting and conceptually plotting the perfect revenge. Buddha called this drinking poison, hoping the enemy would die. I love the phrase about "nursing" anger and resentment which cannot ever heal the patient.

The Bible has many passages about the need to control this volatile emotion. The advice to "keep your temper under control; it is foolish to harbor a grudge," was certainly sound (Ecclesiastes 7:9.) The *Qur'an* states, "The strongest among you is the one who controls his anger." Muhammad (s.a.w.s)

I knew immediately beginning my study of anger that the solutions were worth all the time and effort I could bring to them. I wanted this skill and desperately needed it. At home alone, sometimes, my anger seemed to be all over me.

So, in my studies of this debilitating horror, I read that it would be beneficial to identify those things which "trigger" this emotion. I found the first one in minutes. I can sum this waiting, potential dynamite in one sentence, "A deal's a deal."

But the saddest incidence of my insisting that someone stick to their "deal" with me was in the case of my one and only husband. No matter what, I insisted, we were married "until death do we part." I was in terrible shape emotionally, poor in physical health, and very uncertain how I should manifest my role as his wife. I probably suffered from even more unhealthy mental reactions which caused this poor man to leave me after less than two years.

Further reading revealed that the lack of patience is a real catalyst for my rages. If I would wait until a customer service employee finished their sentence, maybe I would realize then I no longer had a reason to be angry. In this pause, I might recognize that person had solved my complaint.

I believe there have been many times You rendered me speechless out of Your love for the person I wanted to say something dreadful. I know You have helped me with this negative emotion many times. Previously I was just too unhappily entrenched in self-reliance rather than consulting You to deal with this feeling.

I read that sometimes it takes enormous effort to hold on to something, but letting go of that very thing may be even harder. But it is this surrender of the things I cannot change that brings considerable relief. I saw that what I needed was to have more acceptance and submission in my little self. I know You want this as a place to begin the profound change in me.

In the face of my unkindness to myself, You have given me a beautiful sentence when I see injustice on someone's part toward me or even when I have just made a mistake. Hearing a sentence within directs me to a calmer state of mind sooner than anything I would have thought possible.

"I'm on your side," to me is unconditional forgiveness right now coupled with the complete understanding of this negative, failure-caused, emotional moment. Somehow speaking to me as though I had a separate self, comforting my feelings feels right and makes this sentence a huge pain-relieving salve.

Because I am born of You, my true nature is not anger. Anger is not who I am. No wonder I feel so miserable when this feeling has taken over my whole mind and body.

The thought of being kind to myself in the face of my mental unkindness is undoubtedly part of Your wisdom. I believe You gave me that sentence. I suspect You *may even have said it first.*

To counteract the suffering of anger, I had to learn the skill of forgiveness. I don't even remember hearing when I was little about someone my parents had forgiven. So, I started my study of this topic with shallow understanding. I knew what the word meant.

Of course, I heard lots about it in the chapel every morning, and *Bible* classes contained masses amounts of it. I dearly loved the story of Joseph in *Genesis.* He was my hero. Sometimes I just felt gratitude for this meaningful story about Joseph and all his suffering. I know just as Joseph did what it is like to love your parents and siblings no matter what happens into the rest of one's life.

Many writers have written that anger cannot exist if I realize the truth about this person. They have suffered as much as I have and maybe more. Hurtful people must have experienced and are experiencing emotional pain. They probably have said something truly unkind to themselves about themselves.

In my forgiveness study, I have gone to a lot of different religions. Forgiveness has to start with me forgiving me. This we were not taught at home or in school. Forgiveness always seems to be an excellent catalyst to reduce and end the flames of anger.

Momma loved the famous St. Francis prayer. When my niece read this beautiful appeal at her funeral, I cried knowing Momma was hearing that prayer at that moment too. I wonder if I can ever read or say this without her being present.

"Lord, make me an instrument of thy peace.
Where there is hatred, let me sow love.
Where there is injury, pardon.
Where there is doubt, faith.
Where there is despair, hope.
Where there is darkness, light.
Where there is sadness, joy.
O Divine Master,
grant that I may not so much seek to be consoled, as to console;
to be understood, as to understand;
to be loved, as to love;
for it is in giving that we receive,
it is pardoning that we are pardoned,
and it is in dying that we are born to eternal life."

A wise friend taught me higher wisdom in one sentence for how to deal with someone who does things quite differently from me. She said, in effect, I do not have to try to change another person's behavior by trying to enforce upon this person my rules for how she should treat me. Her priceless sentence was, "Lower the bar." In that sentence, I heard the kindness, permission, and lack of control over my seemingly-errant friend, which she so deserved because I cared so much about her. Let me never forget in this life to "lower the bar," a sentence I am sure was taught by our mutual Professor, the loving You.

My spiritual advisor was an enormous help to revisit many memories safely. I went back in my mind and painted all the minutes of unhappiness red as roses with love. You teach me to remember often how much I was given and received which cured an enormous amount of unhappiness from the early life I had stored within me.

With Your presence perhaps I can create a life of eternal forgiveness and be free of anger recognizing every person as having been created by You and therefore worthy of my kindness. You taught me the word "stumbled" to describe mistakes, no matter how severe. That word, to me, is packed with forgiveness.

You taught me even more. From death row to skid row, when I am in a loving moment, I know all these people did was stumble. That is a brand-new view of them as well as myself.

For years I imagined You were disappointed in me. I pictured Your face as sad. I am forever grateful You showed me that this sad expression is impossible for You. You invented forgiveness, and You have never had to revisit it.

Happy and Unhappy World from You

15

I have a friend who never says anything nice about You because You did not create a happy world in which all of us could live blissfully ever after. She reasoned You had the power to do that.

When I started to have some form of maturity, I realized no one had promised me a wonderful life. I knew so many people who had suffered profoundly. How could I be an exception? Now that I see suffering as universal, I can look for what happened as a result of my life as the stage platform of infinite wisdom from You.

I gather the ego causes problems over and over and then experiences glee in trying to figure out how to solve these difficulties. I have read it is not my ego which solves these problems. The rescuer is my inner self. The purpose of suffering is to shrink this ego.

What helps me depart from my ego is knowing I do not possess any amount of wisdom that does not come directly from You. I believe I do not have one original thought.

I remember my sister and I repeating together lots of times, "It's an ill wind that doesn't blow somebody some good." As children, we looked for the good and were always happy to discover this in some dark cloud of an event. But later in this life, I saw that sometimes when things went wrong for me, they might benefit another. When I am very sick and consult a doctor, the doctor's revenue increases.

You showed me the wisdom that no one can make me hurt, angry, or vengeful. That concept, when I remember to practice it, makes suffering go away. The reason no one can create these horrible feelings inside me is that they *are* inside me. It is my thoughts that shape my mind in suffering from past, reactionary, unhappy moments.

These sensitive areas are like buttons installed in my mind long ago. When someone pushes one of these dreadful, negative places, I experience all the emotions associated with that distant and adverse memory

So, to avoid future suffering with an effort, I can lessen, in effect, or hopefully with Your help may miraculously remove these buttons from my consciousness. The enormous pain then of this kind is completely abolished.

But You showed me even more. Studing Japanese psychology, I learned suffering while mourning a loved person in one's life at the time of this person's death is very different from what I have seen and experienced in the West. I need to concentrate on this sorrow to the marrow of my bones. I must isolate this sorrow within me to the exclusion of any other thought. People who experience this focus adjust this experience of someone's death in very individual ways and lengths of time.

But, having allowed that intense sorrow to penetrate, then and only then, I must move into this very moment. The only way, as You showed, to effectively do this is by choosing to remain as much as possible in the present where You always are.

From my mother's life, I have an enormous example of suffering. My mother had spent a year of her teenage life in a tuberculosis hospital after her father died of this disease. The irony was that her father was the engineer of the very building in which she was recovering.

At that time, the treatment for tuberculosis was to put all the patients' beds outside on the porch regardless of the season. In the winter, my mother wore gloves, a pull-down wool hat, and bed covers as high to her chin as possible. She experienced friends dying in this hospital. But with friends, my mother ordered vast amounts of metaphysics courses to endure the long time they had to spend in bed in this facility.

I am very grateful to You for teaching my mother metaphysics. I know an enormous number of people who do not want to know that You had created a "kindness" line joining their head and heart lines on their palms that was not on their hands when they were born. I was thrilled when I saw this lovely gift from You on my hands. This line must take up the Dalai Lama's entire palm.

But as my mother taught me, these are reliable tools for growth. I began my trip to a more profound realization of the truth of You. Study of holy books from Eastern cultures prepared me for the oldest teachings of religions.

With the help of these books, I began to read about what substance forms what I refer to as "me." Reading passages describing Your nature were beautiful. I saw Your incredible power combined with enormous love, which I had not realized so thoroughly in my previous religious studies.

There is such a rich world beneath daily occurrences picked up by our senses. I believe on some level we all seek and crave what is invisible. The answer to, "Who am I?" interests all of us.

While reading spiritual and holy books, You have taken me to the greatest book of all, the one that lies within me referred to by Jesus as the Kingdom of Heaven. This book within cannot be tampered with by some outsider, and it cannot be lost or edited many times like some holy books. The discovery of this book meant the whole world to me.

For me, this book within me affirms every religion is correct for the person who believes this particular dogma. Not arguing with someone about their chosen religion makes enormous sense when I think how much more they know about this subject than I ever will. I could not possibly win such an argument or change their beliefs in any way.

You have taught me that every person's inner wisdom, their sense of right and wrong for themselves, should not be challenged, not by me at least. But if I insist on another person's internal sense of what is valid as being entirely incorrect, by the same logic, my inner wisdom is also wrong.

It interests me now that saying my inner wisdom is correct and someone else's is completely wrong is the basis for every war ever fought. It is also the foundation for most other acute dislikes, sometimes ending in death for someone. Acceptance of another's inner wisdom as being right for this person is higher wisdom and results in inner peace for me.

I do not want to live this life as though my inner wisdom is the only one correct. I want to practice religious tolerance coming straight from You. In this practice, I believe I am right with You.

As I realize I am so close to You, seeing my little life and now my little self as Yours, the ego shrinks. You have taught me that being within my ego mentally and Your presence never connect at the same moment. But You have taught me my ego can be a useful guide in training me to be Home, to finally realize I have always been right Here.

Our Birth is but a sleep and a forgetting:
The Soul that rises with us, our life's Star,
Hath had elsewhere its setting,
And cometh from afar:
Not in entire forgetfulness,
And not in utter nakedness,
But trailing clouds of glory do we come
From God, who is our home:
Heaven lies about us in our infancy!
~William Wordsworth

Trailing Clouds of Glory
at Birth and at Death

9/11 For Us All

16

I was going into the Parish Office where I worked. For some reason, I looked at the majestic twin towers. I never did that. But somewhere inside I must have known that this very morning and the days and weeks which followed would be about nothing less than these monuments.

It was a minor voting day in New York City that Tuesday. The voting booths for that part of the city were in this church's gym. I can't imagine that there were many voters, but these volunteers were there for the day.

I hadn't been at my desk very long when I heard one of our priests laugh out loud with real mirth. My experience with this priest was that he didn't have much humor, so I was curious. I went upstairs where he was in front of a television.

I saw nothing humorous. There was a huge airplane sticking out of one of the towers. I forgot all about the priest in the room with me. I was fighting nausea from the very beginning.

It had to be You who told me then and there my job was to get everyone home. The Franciscan Sister with whom I worked lived a few doors down from the Parish House, and all the priests lived here in this building. But one thing at a time.

I charged out of the front door down to the gym. I told those volunteers what little I knew. And then I was adamant they all had to go home. Those of us who have lived in NYC for any length of time know full-well buses and subways shut down completely in city emergencies. Catching a bus or subway seemed remote, but all these people had to try.

My next problem was my nausea. The thought of losing the contents of my stomach in front of other people filled me with horror. And defiling the space next to the holy cathedral was out of the question. I felt helpless, but I had learned years ago that the way to block nausea is to swallow repeatedly over and over. To just never stop swallowing was all I could do.

But sick as I felt I wanted to know more about what was happening to that tower. I went back to the television and the inappropriate mirth of the priest. I saw a lobby with people frantically going every direction. Men were screaming orders that no one seemed to hear, much less obey.

And then for the first time, I heard an awful sound of metal and concrete plummeting to the ground. The television had gone completely black. I realized all the people I had just seen on television were now dead. The building had imploded upon them.

Now I was feeling full panic. I took the stairs down to talk to the Franciscan Sister. She said she was going back to the Convent. She told me to take care because she knew I had no choice but to walk home.

I didn't say anything to the priests who were living in that building so close to the ongoing tragedy. I had no place to put them. My apartment was a studio. But having worked for priests three years, I doubted they would leave their home.

I think it was You who told me to go home then. Walking home was not a problem for me because I lived 22 blocks away. But walking home, I remember silence. That had to be wrong. Every fire-fighter, every police officer, some ministers, and doctors were going down Houston Street with all the alarm sounds and speed they could muster. It could not have been silent.

I walked with people covered with ash. I knew better than to say anything to them. And they, in turn, spoke to no one beside them either. My mind was racing. I felt like my heart had stopped.

When I got back to my apartment building, there was no one out front or in the lobby. I wanted to ask someone for more information, but there was no one to ask. I had abandoned television years ago, and at that time I did not have a radio. I slept face down for many hours, not bothering to undress. At night being undressed would feel vulnerable and just was too frightening.

I reasoned that anything of that scope and obvious preparation could very well be only the beginning. The thought of more attacks, more fear, was just too much.

The next day I walked the 22 blocks to Houston Street intending to go to work. But the police had blocked off Houston Street leading to the church and Parish House. I saw the police, men and women, weeping. There was no way I could ask them for more information. That would be totally insensitive. Later I realized they had not lost a friend. They had lost dozens.

There was nothing to do but go home again. And again no one was visible along my street or in my building. I always wondered about this. You kept us all apart for reasons I do not understand. But I had learned to trust You, so I just continued to my apartment.

I slept and again I did not undress. I had changed clothes that morning. So again, I just slept the night away. It seems odd now, but being totally asleep was not a problem.

There were no working telephones so I could not call even friends nearby. I was so much in the dark about what had happened that first day and the subsequent days. There was no one to ask.

The third day after the attack, again I went downtown hoping to be allowed to go to work. But the Parish House was just too close to the towers for police to let me pass. Police said going to work was not a good enough reason to be let in that area. Maybe they were afraid of people looting those fallen bodies.

As I was going to work the fourth day, I could not cross the street at the end of mine. There was a convoy of trucks that stretched as far as I could see. I knew where they were going by the expressions on the drivers' faces. They looked tired, overwhelmed, and enormously sad.

Finally, there was a break in the trucks, and I rushed to the bus stop two streets away. There was a sign on the meter of the bus that said "Free." I didn't speak to anyone on the bus. No one was talking to anyone else. We were all locked in our mutual fear and sadness.

This time nothing blocked my way, and I made it to the Parish House. The sister I knew so well was in tears. When she told me what had happened in the last 4 days, I was in tears too. We had never cried in each other's presence, but I didn't even notice we were doing that now.

The days that followed seemed to me to be just as bad as those going before. Like every other church, funerals were all we did. Catholics believe that when one dies, one is given their restored body to enter heaven. Almost all firefighters and police were Catholic. No one could comfort these people who mourned those they loved with the devastation that the murdered people were without bodies.

It was enough to make sure the priest officiating at the funeral knew the name of the person they were honoring. Nothing else seemed possible. A lot more was necessary, but this tiny fact was all we had. I had been overwhelmed seeing the police cry, but now I was surrounded by people who were beyond comfort. There was nothing I could think of to say to them. Saying: "I'm so sorry" felt lame and useless.

A friend told me much later that the day after that horrible Tuesday, she went to a Catholic service. The priest encouraged everyone to forgive their enemies. I realize that those of us who aspire to this noble thought need to do our best to always treat others who cannot with the utmost understanding and care. These people who have lost someone close to them certainly may not be in a position to forgive terrorists.

I don't remember when we crawled back to "normal." It was a very long time. And I don't think any of us still alive will ever be the same person we had been. The terrorists had changed us. But that was their goal.

You pulled us all to safety those remaining alive. And I know how much You comforted individuals. Those who lost their lives are eternal. This horror was also our mandate to grow and change. Nothing You ever do is for nothing. That fact I know. But Your reasons behind this attack are way above my paygrade.

*Cat Found it Necessary
to Swear in All Guests*

Death as I Understand It

17

*B*ecause You taught me about death, I have lost my fear of this "change of address." Those nights when I sleep well, so deeply that I have no sense of me at all, in a similar state of surrender and trust, I involuntarily come to Thee in core sleep. I think this state is very similar to death, and it may be death itself.

But I do not wake up traumatized and miserable, these mornings after a temporary deep sleep. If this form of sleep is a kind of death, no one should be afraid of the final one for this life.

I notice those nights when I do not get deep sleep, I wake up tired and out of energy. I believe if for some reason I cannot surrender, I do not experience a sense of refreshment feeling the intensity of You and Your love.

When I was born, I fell into a caring doctor's arms. I want everyone to know how wonderful it must be falling into the arms of You who is someone so familiar. I want to wrap those persons who are afraid of death in my lowly arms and convince all these people that nothing bad is going to happen when they die.

I believe death is a happy occasion because when I fall into Your arms, I can finally experience the whole of You. It is this body which blocks me from You from experiencing the fullness of You and Your immense love.

I came from You. I return to You. Dying is a natural thing. Being certain of reincarnation means I've done it before. The body is constructed to wear out. There is no reason to be afraid or anxious about something I may be doing many nights.

But You taught me even more. Thanks to You, I have lived with, learned volumes from and loved intensely eight guru-like cats over five decades. Previous to my eighth guru, I did not realize how human a cat can be. For whatever reason, I ended being nuts about this most recent cat.

But, for the first time in this life with cat roommates, You gave me a warning that this eighth cat and I had a limited time left in our mutual company. What struck me the most when this thought appeared and reoccurred was that cat was not even sick.

The death of this cat hit hard. The night he died, I took everything I thought would remind me of him to the dumpster outside my apartment and threw all these things inside. In temporary insanity, I thought not seeing the things this cat loved would make mourning for him less painful.

But, when the full force of the sadness of being without him descended on my mind that night, I remembered a sentence from one of Your holy books, "Neither for the living nor for the dead do the wise grieve." (1) That sentence sustained me for the nights and days that followed.

With Your help, I understood what I loved so much about every cat was the loving self within them which was so visible. Just like the self of all persons within, this self is made entirely of love, the love that is You. Love from You and of You cannot ever die.

(1) From The Bhagavad Gita (2.11) translated into English by Swami Nikhilananda and published by the Ramakrishna-Vivekananda Center of New York; Copyright 1944 by Swami Nikhilananda.

Your Teachings of Oneness

18

In Your holy books and spiritual writing, particularly in Eastern religions, You stress the need for being with spiritually dedicated people to ensure that the spiritual level I have attained strengthens and grows.

And yet, over and over You seem to take me away from whatever holy company I have found.

My first holy company was the teachers in a religious high school I attended for three years. In the chapel, five mornings a week, I kept thinking, "I don't think so." I listened to that sentence with intensity and tried to remember what had invoked that thought.

I came away with conclusions about You that I knew were exclusively for me. Even then You taught me You did not want me to try to change other people's inner wisdom as though only mine were correct.

At my request and after brief study with a minister of my high school's faith, a bishop laid his hands on my head. But the bishop's pronouncement of my intended-forever religion disappeared in my consciousness as quickly as it arrived.

Looking back, so often I imagined You were disappointed in me for my decisions to work for companies I knew nothing about and hasty social choices, too numerous to even recall. I was reacting to every stimulus.

You had introduced me to many men via letters and emails who were versed in Sanskrit and Vedanta Hinduism. I assumed You meant all these teachers as the holy company You stressed in so many spiritual books. But. with two exceptions, I was never in their presence.

It took me quite a while to realize that my chosen teachers from all over the world were not intended as the holy company for the remainder of this life the way I had believed. You eliminated all of them after eight years with a single sentence, "It's a man's religion." Looking back, I had put all these learned men ahead of and above You.

Over these retirement years I believe with all my mind and heart that when I heard something within my mind that I did not know, and it was a new, previously unthought sentence, it had to be from You.

Over many years I have watched myself and others have what is euphemistically called an aha moment. But now I reason that if I didn't have a concept in my mind, how could a millisecond later I believe that same mind conjured this still unknown thought.

It seemed to me in Our awareness that the reason I was having so much difficulty practicing the presence of You per Brother Lawrence's faith was that I was so reluctant to share my space in body and mind. Later that same year, I heard within what I know to be sharing from You, "I haven't moved, and neither have you." I have clung to that sentence ever since.

But it is You and I who inhabit this body's thought and gesture. For years, I have lamented every clumsy moment I drop or fumble something. But now I see all that as gentle nudges from You to return mentally back to the present and repeat my Sanskrit mantra. Mindfulness is still something I struggle to achieve. Having Your help makes everything better.

You taught me early this life that those people who do not believe in You at all, and who think anyone who does is a Fruit-Loop piece of cereal, You love them as much as You love me. I gather being anonymous and appearing as coincidence are two of Your favorite outfits. And even as a tiny child, I saw You as the only one I had experienced who was fair to us all. Your love as quality and quantity never varied. That's why I was nuts about You from the very start.

In retirement, I have read many books on the subject of nonduality. What I have discovered is the intellectual level of this concept as one's new reality. I do not think experience has been a good teacher. For me, experience has been the only teacher.

But You have taught me that it is the experience of realization of You that is what I have as a goal. I do not think I invented and chose this goal for me any more than I choose its path. I believe You have done both.

A teacher of more than 100 years ago gave the enlightenment analogy of a salt doll going into the ocean to come back to tell others the experience of the ocean's depth. And of course, the salt doll dissolves and becomes part of that ocean. Like the salt doll, no spiritual seeker who experiences the depths of You, the Ocean, can come back to tell other devotees what this experience is as they discovered it. From all I have read, the enlightened still around do not talk about this first moment.

In my limited mind, I practice qualified nonduality, which is having an awareness of You distinct from me. But as Your teaching continues, I feel more and more an integral part of You, happy to be Your closest servant, Your ardent devotee, Your best friend within me. I never imagined living within such a beautiful place.

There are many paths I can follow that You have taught. I can perform all action, even this writing, with the thought that I want to make this action the very best I can. In service to You, I take no credit for the results. Turning over all results to You frees me to act idyllically.

You taught through Narendar, an excellent teacher of the 19th century that giving a gift or a kindness wanting something in return like thanks or praise is really "shop-keeping." I am in this instance giving to get. I found this spiritual practice helpful with so many people unable to even say thanks.

After my horrible experience years ago on a prayer mat when I was meditating twice a day, I no longer feel comfortable in formal meditation. I directly go right into a state of mental fear, if not panic, when I sit with a straight spine before Your Altar, which I still have in this apartment.

Even though I cannot meditate, I can sit with You in silence. But sitting quietly with You is still very hard for me to do. I tend to get right up after a very few minutes having had a compelling thought of something that I need to do right away. I know You well enough to know You understand a lot more about that disgusting habit of leaving You in minutes than I ever will.

I stumbled over a passage in one of Your holy books that brought me to tears. "Sometimes the devotee acts as the magnet and God as the needle. Such is the attraction of the devotee that God comes to him, unable to resist his love." (1) That is almost more precious than I can take in to my inner self.

When You were teaching me Haiku poetry, I wrote, "Your Love makes me whole. Without You, I am not me. Thank You for Your Trust." But writing the ending word of "trust" wasn't my idea. My ending word was "Truth." It is an entirely new thought that You trust me. Without You, I am not me. And You seem to be saying You know that I will remember My oneness with You. You have taught me to pay attention to words I did not intend to write. Once I wrote "bood" instead of "book." Bood is sitting quietly with You, and I want to do this.

But it is trust that is at the core of the willingness to give up my sense of a separate self, and like the salt doll disappear into You. I went on the write the Haiku poem, "I adore You so... it is no wonder I feel. . . more love for You now." And that doll is precisely what merging with You is. I feel love for You in awareness of being right with You. There is no space between Us.

Saints must have eliminated their egos early. The holy books, it seems to me, must have been written by those who were either enormously close to You or You wrote the books where later the "author" had merged with You. And like Joan of Arc, their message was, "I am not afraid. I was born to do this."

Once I imagined that every person is part of a beautiful quilt stretching the length and breadth of the whole world. To me, people in this one quilt are different colored yarns – some blue or black, white or gold, with every color that exists. For this quilt to be truly beautiful, all of us have to be in there.

You have shown me the writings of so many excellent teachers to learn higher wisdom. Buddha taught right living, and Jesus taught to love even our enemies combined with knowing the peace within as the Kingdom of God. Both those teachers taught duality, qualified nonduality, and nonduality.

I have lived in a body that experiences everything my senses pick up as being completely detached from me. Sometimes this isolated concept is the duality where I still live. This separation is the state of mind where I experience fear. But in qualified nonduality, I realize You are everything in my world, and my only goal is love and service to You. In qualified nonduality taught by Vedanta Hinduism, everything that I label I experience as You.

Narendra wrote he believed the first five verses of the *Gospel of John (NIV)* was an excellent summation of Christianity.

"In the beginning was the Word, and the Word was with God,
and the Word was God.
He was with God in the beginning.
Through Him all things were made; without Him
nothing was made that has been made.

In Him was life, and that life was the Light of all mankind. The Light shines in the darkness, and the darkness has not overcome it."

The "Him" written in this *Gospel* is Jesus, the beautiful Light for us all. References to this Oneness are all through *The Bible.*

Perhaps this can also mean, In the beginning was the Word, and the Word was with Jesus, and the Word was Jesus. Jesus was with God in the beginning. Through Jesus, all things were made; without Jesus, nothing was made that has been made. In Jesus was life, and that life was the Light of all humanity. The Light of Jesus shines in the darkness, and the Pharisees and Romans knew Him not.

But when You supplied that last word of "trust" in the first Haiku poem, You knew I did not have this peace within. You understood how much fear is within me at the very thought of merging into some space where no one can tell me what it is.

That's where love comes in. I lose my fear knowing I will experience nothing but love with You. I can't even experience the smallest fear in this absorption in You. There is never a reason to fear being in Your love.

(1) From The Gospel of Sri Ramakrishna (page 471) translated into English by Swami Nikhilananda and published by the Ramakrishna-Vivekananda Center of New York; Copyright 1942 by Swami Nikhilananda.

Seeing You Over a Lifetime

19

*M*y father took a photograph of me when I was about one month old. In this picture, my brows look furrowed, and the rest of my face shows fear and panic. Right from the beginning, I seemed to be asking, "Are we sure about this?" I do not believe I was depressed at one month old. But I was disoriented for some reason a lot of this life. I have never thought I was in my real home in any sense of the word. If this were home, why does everyone eventually leave?

I remember departing from You when I was weeping into my horse's mane a year after Popa's death. My beloved sister had been sent away to boarding school, and I missed her terribly. The only consolations I had was when she came home on vacations. For the next six years, I would attempt to take care of my mother without even thinking of asking for Your Help.

For some reason, I formed a conclusion that day leaning on my horse. I believed You had relegated every single thing that needed doing to "the women." As a female of 11 years old, I felt entirely unqualified to do anything of the kind.

My dominant feelings did not leave my mind for half a lifetime. I experienced this worry being alone with my sad mother, a dog, and a horse on a 525- acre farm. I tried to tell no one. I certainly did not tell You.

In mental trouble in my 20's caused by immaturity and bipolar disorder, I went to psychiatrists, all Western in their practice. Instead of assessing what already I possessed in education, jobs, and virtues, they asked questions about previous years ad nauseum. I began to question how understanding my life previously experienced could help me now. It was that past that put me in the first place in these chairs facing these doctors.

Years later guided by You, I studied Eastern psychology on the subject of human psychological change. I took hope in establishing in my mind what experience on many subjects I already possessed. I went back to college for a degree in accounting, graduating when I was 39 years old.

Now knowing my strengths come from You, I can look back and realize all the doctors accomplished was to make me very glad this life is not eternal. I am enormously grateful *You are.*

Often as an adult in my 30's, my closest friend and I talked of You, speculating what You think, feel, and do. She found the sentence: "Love is the answer, now tell me the question." We both loved that thought and tried to apply it to our lives.

Beginning with library books, I started an intense search of world-wide religions with books written by Leo Tolstoy, Albert Einstein, and Albert Schweitzer. I understood as I read their devotion to their beliefs how dedicated adherence to Your Laws and You had shaped and governed their compassionate lives. I wanted the relationship to You I believed these men already had at the time of writing their books.

I started attending lectures about You in an Eastern Religion class consisting of the oldest study of religion in recorded history. Looking back at the sheer number and volumes of those underlined books, I am surprised by the amount of energy I had to devour these previously studied books. I loved the subject of You and read everything I could.

After almost forty years of reading about religions all over the world, it seemed to me, we are all loving, worshiping, and serving the same You.

We each name You and the path we are on in our native languages. I love the wisdom that we all smile in the same language.

This Eastern religion teacher taught me to meditate using a Sanskrit holy word. Once when I was meditating, I experienced what I have always thought of as "myself" become lower than my head settling at the level of my waist. I always believed "me" resided in my head.

At the time I was very nervous "I" would stay at my waist. I was very unsure about how I would handle such a bizarre thing. I had no training in this. But You took it away in minutes.

But here You started teaching me I am not the "me" I think I am. I am consciousness. I am "she" who is aware. This knowledge is another reason not to fear death. This "I" is that is consciousness itself certainly is not going to cease to exist.

I realize over and over how much You helped, counseled, saved, and loved us all. But it took me years to get back to a reciprocal awareness with You, more years than I want to remember. But "back" You brought me in Our retirement years to the space of Our oneness that has always been our Home.

I imagined that I was a separate self when in fact all this life I have been with You. I treasure the last two years learning who I am and where I will always be. My Beloved, I had no idea I was always part of You. I know now I have always been Home. You have taught me in Our oneness I cannot pick You as a flower without touching You at the same moment as a star.

O my Beloved, my love, my very own, the most wonderful teaching You have ever given to me is to see You everywhere, in every person I meet, in every moment of this life, and to know that I am never separated from You. You have never left me, and I know now within I never left You.

With love, friendship and devotion,

Your little self, Vicky

Printed in the United States
By Bookmasters